DRUGS AND BIRTH DEFECTS

It is a pregnant woman's responsibility to provide a healthy and drug-free environment for her unborn child.

THE DRUG ABUSE PREVENTION LIBRARY

DRUGS AND BIRTH DEFECTS

Nancy Shniderman
Sue Hurwitz

THE ROSEN PUBLISHING GROUP, INC.
NEW YORK

TO MY PARENTS
Sue and Gene
N.S.
TO MY CHILDREN
Nancy, Janie, Annie, Stephen, Jeff, and Ron
S.H.

The people pictured in this book are only models. They in no way practice or endorse the activities illustrated. Captions serve only to explain the subjects of photographs and do not in any way imply a connection between the real-life models and the staged situations. News agency photos are exceptions.

Published in 1993, 1995, 1998 by the Rosen Publishing Group, Inc.
29 East 21st Street, New York, NY 10010

Revised 1998

Library of Congress Cataloging-in-Publication Data

Shniderman, Nancy, 1956–.
    Drugs and birth defects / Nancy Shniderman, Sue Hurwitz
        p.   cm. — (The Drug abuse prevention library)
    Includes bibliographical references and index.
    Summary: Explains the dangers that various drugs can pose to pregnant
        women and their unborn children, discussing birth defects such as
        fetal alcohol syndrome and the effects of cocaine and heroin.
    ISBN 0-8239-2621-4
    1. Substance abuse in pregnancy—Juvenile literature. 2. Abnormalities,
        Human—Etiology—Juvenile literature. 3. Fetus—Effect of drugs on—
        Juvenile literature. [1. Fetus—Effect of drugs on. 2. Pregnancy. 3.
        Drugs. 4. Drug abuse.] I. Hurwitz, Sue, 1934–. II. Title. III. Series.
    HV580.S75S56   1993
    618.3'2—dc20   93-9699
                                                                    CIP
                                                                    AC

Manufactured in the United States of America

Contents

Introduction

*E*ach year in the United States, 150,000 babies are born with birth defects. A baby born with birth defects suffers from a mental or physical abnormality. Birth defects are caused by different factors. Sometimes birth defects occur because the mother is very young or because she has not received proper prenatal (before-birth) care. Birth defects might also occur if the mother or father has a sexually transmitted disease. And thousands of birth defects are the result of substance abuse by either or both of the parents at any time during the pregnancy.

Doctors believe that drug use by fathers affects babies, as well as that of mothers. For instance, babies born to fathers who smoke are more likely to have spinal defects. However, the relation between a father's drug use and his child's health is difficult to study. As a result, much more is known about what a mother's drug use can do to the fetus while it is in the womb.

Babies exposed to drugs while in the womb are often born too early and need special care. The brain of a drug-exposed baby develops more slowly in the womb, and brain damage can occur. Upon birth, a drug-exposed baby will experience withdrawal symptoms from the drug, or neonatal abstinence syndrome (NAS). A drug-exposed baby can develop behavior problems as well as physical symptoms, including general weakness, muscle tension, trembling, drowsiness, and hallucinations. A drug-exposed baby is also at higher risk for sudden infant death syndrome (SIDS).

Both illegal drugs, such as cocaine, crack or heroin, and legal drugs, such as alcohol or tobacco, can lead to dangerous results for unborn babies.

It is difficult to accurately estimate how many babies are born exposed to drugs. Many studies focus on urban areas and do not reflect the situation in the rest of the country. In addition, studies rely on a parent reporting his or her own drug use. This leads researchers to believe that the number of babies born exposed to drugs is underestimated. Still, studies report that

8 there are between 100,000 and 740,000 babies born exposed to drugs in the United States every year.

Babies born with birth defects are expensive to care for. The baby and the mother must stay in the hospital longer than usual. The baby needs more medical care. Long-term costs can include special educational needs and foster care placement.

Unfortunately, many drug-abusing parents are unprepared to care for an infant suffering from birth defects. Babies born to substance-abusing parents are often taken away and put with other families. Barry Lester, professor of pediatrics at Brown University, says, "A baby that isn't cuddly can turn off a parent." Reports show that these issues can cause poor parenting and create more problems.

It's important to understand the risks of drug abuse during pregnancy for many reasons. If you're pregnant and using drugs, you need to know that the baby can be born with serious birth defects. The sooner you stop drug use, the better chance your baby will have for a healthy life. You or a sibling may have been born with a birth defect because one of your parents used drugs. Knowing the facts can help you through difficult times and give you some answers. You will learn how to keep your future children safe from drug-related birth defects.

CHAPTER 1

Drugs That Affect Babies

A ny drug that is taken by a pregnant woman will affect the baby. The baby is connected to the mother by an organ called the placenta, through which the baby is nourished. When the mother takes a drug, the baby takes it too. Studies show that each year 2 to 3 percent of newborns are exposed to cocaine, 12 percent are exposed to marijuana and 38 percent to tobacco.

Alcohol and Birth Defects
Alcohol is the most widely used and abused drug in the United States. It causes the most children to have birth defects.

When a mother or a father abuses drugs, they endanger the life of their child. Being a parent means being responsible for another life.

Every mother faces the risk of miscarriage or stillbirth (when a baby is

10 | born dead). Those risks are even greater if a mother uses both alcohol and tobacco during pregnancy.

When a pregnant woman uses alcohol, the alcohol passes freely from her body to her unborn baby's body. The baby gets a powerful dose of alcohol. It affects all of the baby's tiny, developing organ systems.

Doctors have studied babies born to women who drank heavily during their pregnancy. They found that many were born with physical and mental defects. These birth defects are called the *fetal alcohol syndrome*.

Babies who have fetal alcohol syndrome (FAS) are often shorter and weigh less than normal babies. Newborns with FAS are usually irritable. They often have trouble feeding. They become upset easily by light or noise.

FAS babies have very small heads, and they may not look normal. They may have heart defects. They may have joint and limb defects. They also may have poor control of their muscles, which makes them seem clumsy. More than half of these babies have hearing problems.

More than half of FAS babies also have a damaged central nervous system. That often makes them more active than normal. Sometimes these children don't remember things. They may be very nervous. And they may have learning problems later in school.

FAS is one of the leading causes of mental retardation in the United States. It affects about one in every 500 babies born in this country today.

Sometimes babies are born with only some of the fetal alcohol syndrome birth defects. They are said to have *alcohol-related birth defects*. Many more babies are born with alcohol-related birth defects than with the more serious defects of FAS.

High levels of alcohol are necessary to produce all the birth defects of fetal alcohol syndrome. But babies whose mothers drink smaller amounts of alcohol may have some alcohol-related birth defects.

Doctors do not know how much alcohol it takes to harm a baby. But they do know that the more alcohol is used, the greater the danger is to a baby.

In 1981 the Surgeon General of the United States warned pregnant women about drinking. He also warned them to watch the alcohol content of foods and drugs. But many pregnant women still drink enough to injure an unborn baby.

12 The safest choice a pregnant woman can make is to use no alcohol at all. That is safest for her baby. That is also safest for her own body.

A woman can prevent fetal alcohol syndrome and alcohol-related birth defects in her child if she does not use any alcohol during pregnancy.

She owes that to her baby. She owes that to herself.

Tobacco and Birth Defects

More than 56 million people use tobacco in the United States today. According to the World Health Organization about 3 million people worldwide die each year as a result of smoking.

Nicotine is a colorless, oily chemical in tobacco. Nicotine is habit-forming. Large doses of nicotine can kill you. Tar is another chemical in tobacco. Tar is the brownish, sticky stuff that smokers sometimes get on their fingers. Tar can cause cancer.

Carbon monoxide, cyanide, and lead are poisons found in tobacco smoke. They are dangerous to a smoker and to everyone around the smoker.

In fact, long-term abuse of tobacco can cause emphysema (a lung disease) and bronchitis (a breathing disease). It can

It is best to abstain from cigarettes or any other drugs during pregnancy.

14 also cause heart disease and cancer of the lungs, mouth, larynx, and esophagus. Using smokeless tobacco, snuff, or low-tar cigarettes does not lower those dangers.

Pregnant women who use tobacco often deliver babies that weigh less than normal. The less a baby weighs at birth, the greater the chance of its dying or being very sick. Infants born to women who smoked during pregnancy are also more likely to die of sudden infant death syndrome (SIDS), or crib death. SIDS is when babies die quickly and for no apparent reason.

The risk of low birth weight increases with the amount of tobacco used each day. If a mother quits smoking by the fourth month of pregnancy, her chances of having a low-birth-weight baby are probably no greater than those of a nonsmoker.

Marijuana and Birth Defects

Marijuana is a drug made from a plant called *Cannabis sativa*. There are over 400 chemicals in this plant, but the main mind-changing chemical is THC (1-delta-9-tetrahydrocannabinol). A marijuana joint is made from the dried plant.

Marijuana smoke contains more cancer-causing chemicals than tobacco. Users often inhale marijuana smoke deeply. They hold it in their lungs as long as possible. This is extremely harmful and dangerous for the smoker, often damaging the lungs.

Smoking marijuana raises the amount of carbon monoxide in the blood. Carbon monoxide increases heart rate and blood pressure. This decreases the amount of blood that passes from a pregnant woman to her baby.

A baby gets oxygen through the blood flow from its mother. When she uses marijuana, less blood goes to her baby. Then her baby doesn't get the oxygen it needs to grow normally.

Using tobacco also lowers the amount of blood that passes from a mother to her baby. But tobacco is not inhaled as deeply as marijuana, so it is not as harmful to the baby. Smoking marijuana puts five times more carbon monoxide into a mother's bloodstream than smoking tobacco.

The chemicals from smoking even one joint may take as long as 30 days to leave a user's body. That exposes an unborn baby to dangerous chemicals for a long time.

Using marijuana during pregnancy may cause the baby to be born early and have low birth weight. As we know, that is not healthy for a baby.

16 | ### *Cocaine and Crack and Birth Defects*

Cocaine is one of the most habit-forming drugs of abuse. It is a drug that can kill, and kill quickly.

Cocaine is made from the leaves of the coca plant, which grows in South America. It is usually made into a fine white powder that looks like flour or sugar. Cocaine can be snorted through the nose, injected into a vein, or smoked.

Crack is the street name for the cocaine that comes in large white crystals. The name *crack* comes from the crackling sound made when this form of cocaine is smoked. Crack is absorbed into a smoker's lungs quickly.

Crack has become a big problem in most American cities because it is cheap. Crack is very habit-forming. Users often crave crack after trying it just once or twice.

Cocaine affects the central nervous system, including the brain. It speeds up a user's heart rate. It tightens the blood vessels, which raises the blood pressure. Less oxygen reaches the brain. These physical changes may lead to seizures (fits), mental problems, heart attacks, or strokes.

Cocaine use during pregnancy may cut off oxygen to the unborn child. Decreased oxygen can cause low birth weight and smaller-than-normal babies. These babies often have smaller-than-normal heads. A small head may not let a baby's brain develop normally.

17

Use of crack and cocaine during pregnancy is harmful for both mother and baby.

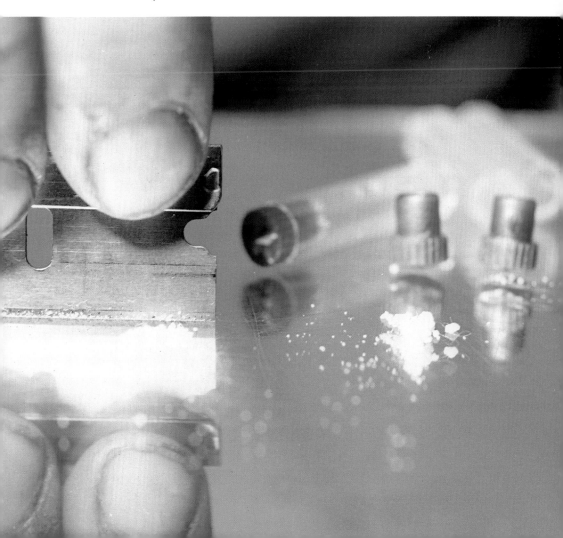

"Crack babies" are born addicted to cocaine. Some of them die soon after birth. They may have seizures before birth or after they are born. These babies are often weak and at a greater risk for SIDS.

Many crack babies have damaged nervous systems. They do not adjust easily to things around them. They may be irritable. They often do not cuddle or nurse well. It is hard to take care of them.

Cocaine use during pregnancy makes a mother more likely to have seizures or a miscarriage. It also increases her risk of bleeding and of the baby's being born too early.

Some states are beginning to pass laws that will take a baby away from its new mother if her urine tests positive for cocaine. Lawmakers believe that a drug addict is not capable of caring for a crack baby, who is often very sick and needs lots of medical and parental attention. They think it is child abuse when a baby is born with cocaine in its system or shows signs of withdrawal. Lawmakers want laws to protect these babies until their mothers stop taking drugs and are more able to take good care of them.

Drug use during pregnancy may cause miscarriage and other severe health problems.

20 | ### *Heroin and Birth Defects*

Heroin is one of a group of drugs called narcotics. Heroin is responsible for 90 percent of the narcotic abuse in the United States.

Heroin is made from opium, which is found in the poppy plant grown in warm climates of Asia. Heroin is made into a white or brownish powder. Usually it is dissolved in water and injected.

Pregnant women who have a drug problem can find help in rehabilitation clinics.

Long-term abuse of heroin may cause liver disease, infection of the heart lining, skin sores, and congested lungs. AIDS is also a risk from dirty or shared needles.

Doctors believe that nearly half of the women who use heroin during pregnancy suffer from anemia (weakness caused by not enough red blood cells), heart disease, diabetes (too much sugar in blood and urine), pneumonia, or liver disease.

Pregnant women who use heroin have more miscarriages, early births, and stillbirths. They also have more breech deliveries (when the baby is born feet first).

Babies whose mothers used heroin often have changes in their brain that make them behave differently from normal babies. They do not always react the same way, so it is hard to tell what these babies may do. They usually do not like to be held or comforted. That makes it hard for parents to cuddle and love their babies.

Babies born to heroin users also have withdrawal symptoms that may last weeks or months. Many of them die. These babies are five to ten times more likely than normal babies to die of SIDS.

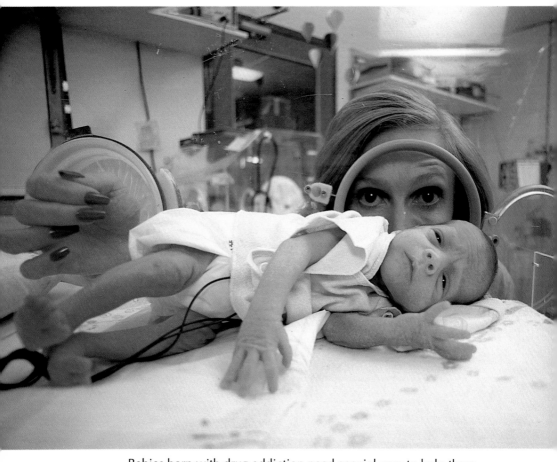

Babies born with drug addiction need special care to help them survive.

The withdrawal symptoms may be diarrhea, cramps, upset stomach, chills, sweating, nausea, vomiting, fever, seizures, uneasiness, and runny nose and eyes. These symptoms cause the babies to lose weight, and often they become very weak.

Heroin-addicted babies are more active and sleep less than normal babies. They have a high-pitched cry. Because they move about a lot, these babies often skin their knees, toes, elbows, and nose on the bedclothes.

Babies born addicted to drugs are at high risk. They are not healthy. They need special medical care after birth. They need extra care when they go home. That makes these babies harder to raise. Parents must make a special effort to take good care of high-risk babies. Laws may soon be passed to see that these babies get the care they need. That may mean taking the babies away from their parents.

A woman who uses drugs is not taking good care of herself or her baby. If a woman is old enough to become a mother, she is old enough to do the right thing. That means staying drug-free and taking good care of her baby.

Alcohol addiction during pregnancy will harm a baby.

CHAPTER 2

How Drugs Cause Birth Defects

While not all women who use drugs during pregnancy have babies with birth defects, there is overwhelming evidence that drug use is dangerous to an unborn baby. Birth defects resulting from drug abuse are completely preventable.

Killian started drinking when she was sixteen. All her friends drank, and she just went along with the crowd. When Killian went off to college, she drank more and more. College seemed like one big party. One night, at a particularly wild party, she met Gabe. He was funny and popular. She really liked him. However, Gabe's drinking wasn't limited to parties, he drank every day. Killian

25

26 *and Gabe started seeing each other all the time, and they drank whenever they were together. Sometimes Killian didn't feel like partying, but Gabe became angry with her when she suggested they do something else.*

At the end of freshman year, Killian became pregnant and decided to keep the baby. Killian's doctor told her to eat healthy foods and take care of herself, but that was difficult to do around Gabe. She ended up drinking during her pregnancy to appease Gabe. He became very upset if she didn't drink with him. Six months into the pregnancy, Killian went into labor. She gave birth three months early. Her baby was born with fetal alcohol effects (FAE). He was underweight and cried for long periods of time. The doctor told Killian that it was more than likely that her baby would suffer considerable mental disabilities due to the FAE.

History of Birth Defects

Fifty years ago, many doctors believed that the baby was protected from any harm as long as he or she was in the uterus. The uterus is the place in a woman's body where the baby develops. Doctors thought that the uterus acted like a glass bubble and kept the baby safe from any outside dangers.

During World War II, however, radiation

from atomic bombs dropped on Japan proved that outside elements could affect an unborn baby. The radiation caused birth defects to babies whose mothers had been in the early stages of their pregnancy when the bombs exploded.

In the 1960s, many pregnant women were prescribed sedatives, such as Valium, in order to relieve stress. The sedatives caused many babies to be born with limb (arm and leg) defects. At this time, doctors told pregnant women to avoid all drugs because they could have a negative effect on the unborn baby. In 1979, the U.S. Surgeon General's report, "Healthy People," found five major risk factors related to a higher incidence of infant death: smoking, alcohol abuse, drug abuse, on-the-job hazards, and injuries.

How Drugs Reach the Baby

When a drug is taken by a pregnant woman, the drug enters her bloodstream. From the blood the drug is transferred to the baby through the placenta. The placenta is directly connected to the baby by the umbilical cord. The umbilical cord transports all substances from the mother to the baby. After passing through the placenta, the drug then travels through the umbilical cord into the baby's entire body.

It takes months of patience and care to help undersized, drug-addicted babies develop and grow.

The baby also receives oxygen through the placenta. In the same way as a drug, cigarette smoke can be passed to the baby. Smoking cigarettes reduces blood flow to the baby while the mother is smoking and for fifteen minutes after. Cigarette smoke speeds up the baby's heart and increases the level of stress hormones in the blood.

When alcohol crosses the placenta, the baby attains a blood alcohol level similar to that found in the mother. Cocaine also readily crosses the placenta and can be found in the baby's blood minutes later. Cocaine narrows the blood vessels and prevents oxygen and other nutrients from reaching the baby. Cocaine remains in the baby's system longer than it remains in the mother's system because the baby's liver is not fully developed. The liver helps cleanse the body of drugs and toxins.

There are three stages of a baby's development. The type of birth defect and how serious its effects are can depend partly on when the baby is exposed to drugs.

The first development stage occurs within the first seventeen days of a baby's life. A baby exposed to drugs during the first stage will most likely result in a miscarriage (when the fetus is expelled from the mother's body before it has developed

30 into a baby that can survive on its own).

The second stage of development happens from day eighteen to day fifty-five of pregnancy. A baby's organs are growing rapidly during this time. At this stage, a drug-exposed baby is at a high risk for organ and limb defects. The final stage occurs from day fifty-six to the time of birth. A baby's eyes and brain are still developing at this stage and can easily be damaged by a mother's substance abuse.

When Amber discovered that she was pregnant, her doctor told her that she had to stop smoking. Amber decided to follow her doctor's advice. It was going to be very hard, but she wanted a healthy baby.

Amber's husband James smoked too. He supported Amber's decision, but he said that he wasn't ready to quit. Amber's pregnancy was very stressful. She found it hard to watch James smoke—it made her crave a cigarette. She was also hurt that James wouldn't quit smoking too. By the time the baby, Carly, was born, Amber and James were having marital problems. They were constantly fighting. Amber demanded that James not smoke around the baby, but he wouldn't listen to her. Months later, she finally decided to leave him and move in with her mother. Amber wanted a healthy environment for Carly.

Babies of drug-addicted mothers are often cared for in special homes or centers.

Counselors or support groups can help pregnant women with their drug-abuse problems.

Shortly after the move, Amber rushed Carly to the hospital because she had stopped breathing in the middle of the night. Carly was saved, but doctors kept her in the hospital for a few days to perform tests. Amber was told that Carly had asthma as a result of being exposed to cigarette smoke and needed special medical care. Amber called James to tell him what happened. James felt awful. He felt guilty for hurting Carly. He promised Amber he would quit smoking and help take care of Carly. Amber could see that he meant what he said. She was upset with him, but thought that Carly needed the love and attention of both parents right now.

33

Drug Exposure After Birth

In addition to being exposed to drugs while in the uterus, a baby can also be affected by drugs after it is born. The baby can be exposed through the mother's breast milk. Also, any kind of smoking near a baby—cigarettes, crack, or marijuana, for example—can be very harmful.

Studies show that infants exposed to cocaine smoke may experience nausea and hallucinations. They may even fall into a coma. Also, a baby exposed to cocaine through breast milk is at risk for seizures, heart attacks, and death.

34   According to a report by the Environ-
mental Protection Agency (EPA), second-
hand cigarette smoke was the cause of
almost 300,000 respiratory infections in
children under the age of two. The
National Center for Health Statistics
reports that babies are twice as likely to
die from SIDS if their mothers stopped
smoking during pregnancy but then
started again after birth.

The greater the exposure, the greater
the risk. If both parents are abusing drugs,
the baby is in even more danger. It's clear
that it is not enough to avoid drugs only
during pregnancy. The best insurance for
a healthy child is to lead a healthy lifestyle
at all times.

CHAPTER 3

Teens and Birth Defects

*R*amona and her friends were hanging out at a party one night. She was depressed because she had recently broken up with her boyfriend. An older guy named Rey started talking to her. Ramona thought he was cute, and she liked the attention he was paying to her. When he pulled out a small vial of cocaine and asked her to try some, she thought, why not? She was tired of feeling down. She wanted to have some fun. So she took a few hits. She felt great—like she could do anything. When Rey asked her to take a ride with him, she didn't hesitate. They left the party and ended up in the back of his van.

36   *Ramona and Rey saw each other many times after that. Ramona started using cocaine on a regular basis. Months later she found out she was pregnant. Ramona wanted to get an abortion, but the clinic told her it was too late. She was already four months pregnant. When Ramona gave birth, her baby's legs were disfigured and his organs were not developed properly. Her cocaine abuse had caused the baby's birth defects.*

Teen Drug Use

Teen drug use is on the rise. Alcohol is the number-one drug problem among teens. Every day 3,000 teens start smoking cigarettes. According to the annual federal report conducted by the U.S. Government, there was a 78 percent increase in illicit drug use among youths age twelve to seventeen between 1992 and 1995. In addition, the report stated that cocaine use was up 166 percent in 1995.

Some experts believe that the main reasons for the increase in teen drug use are a change in attitude toward drugs among teenagers, the glamorization of drug use in fashion, television, and film, and the lack of proper drug education and prevention programs.

Today, teens who use drugs often don't think that their drug use is dangerous. This

Regular physical checkups at a clinic or doctor's office are important for a healthy pregnancy.

38 attitude may be caused partly by a lack of awareness about the harmful affects of drugs. According to the Partnership for a Drug-Free America, there has been a large decline in the amount of drug coverage in the news, as well as fewer public-service announcements about drugs on television, radio, and in newspapers. Without the proper awareness, many teens may believe that drugs are simply a fun and experimental part of their teenage years.

The increase in celebrity drug use has also affected teens' attitudes toward drugs. In rock and rap song lyrics, in music videos, and in fashion magazines, drug use is often portrayed as cool. Popular bands sing about alcohol and marijuana, and trendy films depict stories of drug use in an effort to entertain the teen audience. These messages are not balanced with information on the harmful effects of drugs.

Many teens look up to their favorite actors or musicians. But celebrity drug use is not glamorous—in fact, it can be deadly. Drugs claimed the life of actor River Phoenix at age twenty-three. Robert Downey Jr.'s battle against drug addiction has been well-publicized. Members of bands such as Hole, Smashing Pumpkins, and Stone Temple Pilots have also suffered from drug addiction. While these events should make it clear how dangerous drug abuse can be, pop culture continues to promote drug use.

If you are thinking about taking drugs, or if you are taking drugs right now, it's important to educate yourself about the dangers. Being a teenager in today's fast-paced world is not always easy. But turning to drugs will only make your life worse.

Drug Use and Pregnancy

Drugs alter your personality in many ways. One common effect of drugs is a loss of your inhibitions. Inhibition is an internal force that controls certain activities and expressions. Inhibitions help to protect you. They can act as warning signals to help you decide what you feel comfortable doing.

It may feel good to lose your inhibitions because you may feel more relaxed and confident. But you may end up doing things you wouldn't normally do.

When our inhibitions are gone, we may not fully weigh the consequences of our actions. If Ramona hadn't been using cocaine, she might have been more careful when making decisions about unprotected sex.

When a teenager becomes pregnant, she must make some major decisions. Often the first decision is whether or not to have

Irritable and sick babies are difficult to care for.

the baby. If the teen decides to give birth, she must then figure out if she wants to keep the baby or place him or her for adoption. Many times choices are made based on the amount of emotional and financial support available to the pregnant teen. One thing is always true, however: these are not easy decisions. An unwanted pregnancy can make your life extremely difficult. It is harder to stay in school and get an education. This can make it difficult to find and keep a job.

But if you get pregnant while abusing drugs, your life becomes even more difficult. You now have to worry about the baby being born with birth defects.

The only sure way to prevent pregnancy is to practice abstinence and to not have sex at all. If you decide to be sexually active, practice safer sex by using latex condoms every time.

Preventing birth defects is simple. Doctors recommend staying away from all drugs, legal and illegal, during pregnancy, unless they are prescribed by your doctor. If you are pregnant and using drugs, the best thing you can do is stop immediately. It is best to stop in the earliest stages of pregnancy, but stopping at any time will benefit both you and the baby and increase your chances of having a healthy baby.

42 Research reports show that expectant mothers who stop smoking have positive effects within forty-eight hours. The baby receives 8 percent more oxygen.

You may think that a small amount of drugs will not harm the baby. But even small amounts reach the baby and cause harm. Pregnant women who have one or two drinks a day are twice as likely as nondrinkers to have a baby born with birth defects. You may also be thinking it's okay to use drugs as long as you don't get pregnant. But that's not true.

First of all, even if you are very careful, if you are sexually active you still run the risk of getting pregnant. Like Ramona, you may not realize that you are pregnant for several weeks. You may be engaging in harmful activity while you are pregnant and not know it. An unborn baby is at high risk during the third, fourth, and fifth weeks of pregnancy. If you suspect you are pregnant, don't ignore it or pretend it's not happening. It's crucial to get proper care and medical treatment early in a pregnancy. And it's important to stay drug-free to prevent birth defects. Secondly, using any drug can lead to tolerance and addiction and cause major problems in your life.

A healthful diet during pregnancy will improve the chance of having a healthy baby.

44 | *Drug Addiction*

If you continue taking a drug, your body soon develops a tolerance to it. You need to use more and more of the drug to get the original effect. For example, at first, a couple of drinks may be all you need to feel drunk. But soon you find that you need much more than that to have the same feeling. The longer you use a drug, the more you will need to take to feel its effects. Soon, the drug use becomes a habit. When a person begins to lose control over how much or how often drugs are used, he or she has crossed the line into abuse. Drugs become the driving force in an abuser's life.

With many drugs, the longer a person abuses a drug, the greater the chance that he or she will become addicted. However, it is important to be aware that some drugs, such as heroin, are so highly addictive that you can become addicted just by trying them once. Addiction means being dependent on the drug. The user feels that he or she cannot function without it. When a person is addicted to drugs, he or she cannot stop using. An addict will do anything to get drugs. He will steal, lie, and hurt people, even those who love him.

Addiction results from physical and psychological dependence. Psychological dependence means that a person needs the drug in order to function. An addict believes it's impossible to get through the day without taking the drug. Physical dependence is when a person's body needs the drug and experiences withdrawal symptoms without it. An addict cannot stop using on his or her own. He or she will need professional help to quit.

45

Drug addiction is not easy to overcome. An addiction that starts during the teen years can cause problems later in life when a person may be ready to start a family. The best way to ensure a healthy, productive future is to lead a drug-free life. You will benefit now and for the rest of your life. When you decide it is the right time to have a baby, you and your baby won't have to worry about drug-induced birth defects.

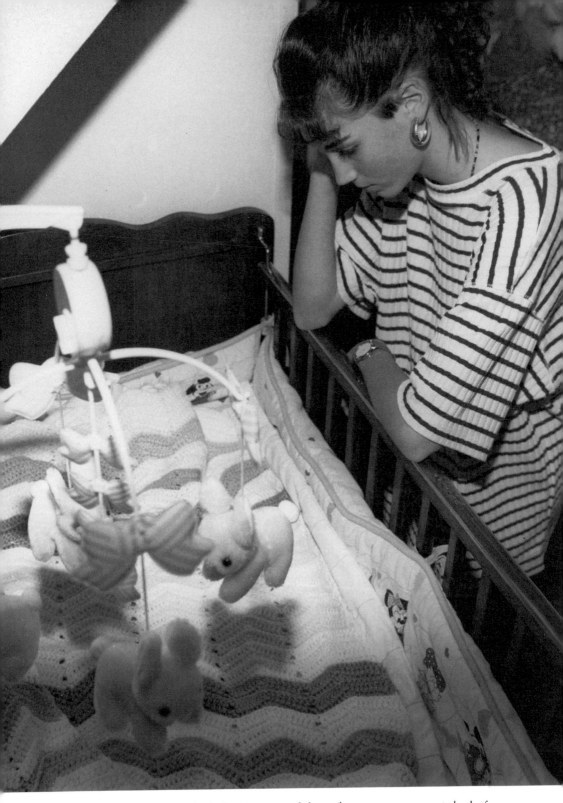

The loss of a baby because of drug abuse causes a great deal of pain and guilt.

CHAPTER 4

Growing Up with Birth Defects

*K*enny *was nervous about starting seventh grade. Not only was he worried about fitting in, but his old guidance counselor recommended that he take some special classes to help him with the harder subjects. A few years before, Kenny had begun having trouble in math and science. His teachers in grade school had been patient, but things would be different now. He was going to a bigger school and his guidance counselor said the teachers couldn't provide him with the individual attention he needed. Kenny didn't understand why these problems were happening to him now.*

When Kenny told his parents what was happening they looked troubled, but they didn't yell at him. He expected them to be

48 *disappointed, but they seemed more upset with themselves. Kenny's mother, Tina, sat him down and told him she was an alcoholic. She had stopped drinking in the first few months of her pregnancy. When Kenny was born with no birth defects, she had thought that everything was okay. But now Kenny had to deal with having a learning disability. He couldn't believe what he was hearing. He was so angry with his mother. He told her he hated her. Why did she have to be so careless?*

Until recently, researchers had little information about the long-term effects of drug abuse. It is known that drug-exposed babies, like Kenny, run a high risk of developing learning disabilities. Unfortunately, not all birth defects are noticeable right away. With FAS in particular, behavior problems and learning disabilities cannot always be diagnosed at birth. The long-term effects of babies born exposed to cocaine have not yet been fully determined either. The most reliable findings, however, show problems with attention span and difficulties with motor skills.

Physical Disabilities

While Kenny suffered from a learning disability, some babies are born smaller or with physical abnormalities. If you or a family member has a physical drug-induced birth defect, it can be difficult to handle the physical and emotional problems that come with being physically challenged.

Life can become increasingly stressful, especially as you enter the teenage years. Most teens want to fit in with their peers. They don't want to stand out or be noticeably different from their friends. But if you are physically challenged, you must learn to deal with your feelings. Sometimes it may seem overwhelming to you, as if your burdens are too much to take. But be aware that there are people who will listen to you and help you with your problems. Reaching out to those who love and support you will give you strength when you need it.

You may feel angry at your parent for causing your birth defect. This is natural. It may be difficult for you to come to terms with your situation right away. As you encounter new challenges, old feelings of anger may come to the surface. It's understandable that you feel this way. But remember, while your parent is responsible for what happened, he or she did not intentionally hurt you.

Drug addiction is a disease, as cancer is a disease. If your parent has successfully recovered from the addiction, it's beneficial for you and your parent to accept what

50 | has happened and move on. Open com-
munication will help both of you deal with
the situation. The help list at the end of
this book will provide you with resources
and organizations specialized in helping
teens with these types of problems. It's
important to also remember that you are
not alone.

Unfortunately, there are many teens
who may be dealing with the long-term
effects of a birth defect. Whether the defect
was caused by drug abuse or other circum-
stances, you can find support from other
teens who understand many of the
experiences that you are going through.

Most importantly, recognize the
importance of having goals and realize
that you can accomplish those goals and
be successful. While you may experience
prejudice because of your disability, you
will also find people who accept and love
you for who you are. The person who
doesn't accept you on the basis of a
disability is the one with the problem, not
you. You are better off without that person.

Neglect

In addition to physical problems, children
may develop poorly because of the
unstable lifestyle caused by a parent's
chemical abuse. If a drug-abusing parent

Medical bills for a sick baby can be overwhelming for a young mother.

52 does not receive help for his or her problem, the child is in danger. Babies born with birth defects require extra attention and care. A parent with a drug problem may not be able to provide that care. In addition to the lack of proper care, a drug-abusing parent may be more likely to physically abuse a child.

The National Committee for Prevention of Child Abuse reports that more than 675,000 children are seriously injured every year by a drug-abusing parent. With proper treatment, however, the parent can recover from his or her addiction and be able to provide a nurturing, supportive environment.

The Law

The Foster Care Social Services Agency is a national system with the purpose to help, protect, and care for endangered children. In the past twenty years, the foster care system has seen a dramatic increase in the number of foster care children. These children are more likely to be victims of FAS, abuse, and crack addiction than children in the past. Today's foster child will stay in foster care longer and may have trouble finding a family who can give him or her the proper care.

According to the National Association of Foster Care Providers, 1,000 of the

4,000 foster children in South Carolina are in special programs due to exposure to substance abuse. In response to this problem, the South Carolina Supreme Court passed a decision that says women who use illegal drugs during their pregnancy can be prosecuted for child abuse. The mother can be sentenced up to ten years in prison for abuse to her unborn baby. This is the first time a court has upheld a prosecution of this kind. Other states may follow this example if the problem continues to increase.

Being born with a birth defect forces you to face special obstacles. You must deal with challenges every day—ones that other people may not have to think about. This does not mean that you cannot live a happy, productive life. It does not mean that you have no control over your future. You are not to blame for what happened, and it may seem unfair that you have to deal with the effects of a birth defect. But you can overcome these obstacles and you will be a stronger person for it.

Being drug-free and responsible during pregnancy gives a mother the best chance to enjoy a healthy child.

CHAPTER 5

Healthy Parents, Healthy Babies

*A*s a parent, or a parent-to-be, it is crucial for you to be honest with your doctors about any potential dangers to which you may have subjected your unborn baby. If drugs were used during your pregnancy the best thing you can do is tell your doctor. Even though you may risk being separated from your child, it is the right thing to do. Both parents should be honest about their drug use. Only when doctors are aware of the full extent of the drug use can they provide the proper treatment. By showing a commitment to the health of your baby, you not only help his or her future, but you increase the chances

56 of keeping and raising your baby.

Effective drug intervention programs for drug-dependent parents and their children are crucial for ensuring the child's development. This includes both the physical and emotional well-being of the child. Often, a social worker is assigned to assess each case. With regular contact to the home to offer assistance, information, and advice, a parent can learn to care for a child exposed to drugs.

Staying Drug-Free

The best choice you can make for yourself is not to use drugs. That may not be an easy choice, but it's one worth making. It is important to participate in drug-free activities and hang out with friends who don't do drugs. Drugs take away any control you have over your life. Before you try any drug, think about what you have to lose. Take responsibility for your life and do something positive that makes you feel good about yourself. Different things work for different people.

Many things can give you enjoyment and fuel your creative spirit. You may choose to participate in a sport, play music in a band, or act in a play. By choosing drug-free activities, you can meet people who like to do similar things. Having drug-free friendships is your best defense against the threat of drugs.

Drugs and the temptation to experiment with them will always be around. But making the choice not to use them will become easier and easier each time you say no. Whether you are pregnant or not, it is smart to lead a healthy lifestyle. By treating your body in a positive way, you are better prepared for your future—especially if that future includes having children.

Glossary
Explaining New Words

addict Person who physically and psychologically needs a habit-forming substance to function and to avoid withdrawal symptoms.

AIDS (Acquired Immune Deficiency Syndrome) A stage of HIV disease when the immune system has been damaged by the virus and is unable to fight infection.

birth defect Mental or physical problem present in a newborn infant.

central nervous system The brain and spinal cord.

dependence The need to take a drug often.

fetal alcohol effects (FAE) The presence of one or more birth defects caused by the mother's alcohol use during pregnancy.

mental retardation Slowness of thought or action; less than normal intelligence.

support group Group of people who provide each other with comfort and courage at meetings through the sharing of similar experiences.

withdrawal symptoms Unpleasant feelings or sickness, such as shaking, headaches, nausea, and nervousness that a person may experience after he or she stops taking a drug.

Where to Go for Help

Al-Anon/Alateen Family Group
  Headquarters, Inc.
1600 Corporate Landing Parkway
Virginia Beach, VA 23454
(800) 356-9996
Web site: http\\:www.al-anon.alateen.org

Coalition on Alcohol and Drug
  Dependent Women and Their Children
Washington Office of NCADD
1511 K Street, NW
Washington, D.C. 20005
(202) 737-8122

March of Dimes Birth Defects
  Foundation
P. O. Box 1657
Wilkes-Barre, PA 18703
(800) 367-6630

60 National Association of Perinatal Addiction
Research Foundation (NAPARE)
11 East Hubbard
Chicago, IL 60611
(800) 638-BABY

National Clearinghouse for Alcohol and
Drug Information
P. O. Box 2345
Rockville, MD 20847
(800) 729-6686
Web site: http\\:www. health.org

National Clearinghouse on Child Abuse and
Neglect Information
P. O. Box 1182
Washington, D.C. 20013
(703) 385-7565

National Families in Action
2296 Henderson Mill Road
Atlanta, GA 30345
(404) 934-6364

For Further Reading

Beyer, Kay. *Coping with Teen Parenting,* rev. ed. New York: The Rosen Publishing Group, 1995.

Brown, Fern G. *Teen Guide to Caring for Your Unborn Baby.* New York: Franklin Watts, 1989.

Corser, Kira. *When the Bough Breaks: Pregnancy and the Legacy of Addiction.* Portland, OR: NewSage Press, 1993.

Dorris, Michael. *The Broken Cord.* New York: Harper Collins, 1990.

Guernsey, JoAnn Bren. *Teen Pregnancy.* New York: Crestwood House, 1989.

Hawksley, Jane. *Teen Guide to Pregnancy, Drugs and Smoking.* New York: Franklin Watts, 1989.

Healthy Women, Healthy Lifestyles: Here's What You Should Know About Alcohol and Other Drugs. United States Dept. of Health and Human Services. Rockville,

62   MD: Substance Abuse and Mental Health Services Administration, 1995.

Lindsay, Jeanne Warren and Jean Brunelli. *Teens Parenting—Your Pregnancy and Newborn Journey: How to Take Care of Yourself and Your Newborn If You're a Pregnant Teen.* Buena Park, CA: Morning Glory Press, 1991.

McCuen, Gary E., editor. *Born Hooked: Poisoned in the Womb,* rev. ed. Hudson, WI: G.E. McCuen Publications, 1994.

Nevitt, Amy. *Fetal Alcohol Syndrome.* New York: The Rosen Publishing Group, 1996.

Stump, Jane Barr. *Our Best Hope: Early Intervention with Prenatally Drug-Exposed Infants and Their Families.* Washington, D.C.: Child Welfare League of America, 1992.

Trapani, Margi. *Listen Up: Teenage Mothers Speak Out.* New York: The Rosen Publishing Group, 1997.

Index

About the Author

Nancy Shniderman has a B.S. in computer science and has taught computer camp for teenagers.

Sue Hurwitz has an M.A. in education and has taught grades K–9. She is the coauthor of a young-adult biography, *Sally Ride: Shooting for the Stars.*

Photo Credits

Cover photo by © Susan Greenwood/Gamma-Liaison; pp. 17, 20 © AP/Wide World Photos; p. 22 © Yvonne Hemsey/ Gamma-Liaison; p. 28 © John Chiasson/Gamma-Liaison; p. 31 © Mike Okoniewski/Gamma-Liaison; all other photos by Stuart Rabinowitz.